Written and illustrated

by

Jane Castle

Cover illustration by Jane Castle and Nada Serafimovic
Cover design by Robin Fight
First published in 1963
© 2021 Jenny Phillips
goodandbeautiful.com

Contents

The Lookout 1

The Squirrel 11

The Swallows 21

The Opossums 30

The Roof. 43

The Lookout

Jay came to his uncle's farm for a visit. Off by the cornfield he saw a big tree and ran to climb it.

When he stood under it, he said to himself, "Why, this tree is as big as a house."

Its leaves were as big as his head. Its flowers were longer than his hands.

As Jay climbed the tree, he could not see out because the leaves were too thick. He felt as if he were in a big tent of leaves. Then he came to a dead branch with only a few leaves. From here he could see out. He saw the house and his aunt Ellen in the vegetable garden.

Jay looked up into the tree. All he could see above was leaves.

"I guess I've climbed about halfway," he said.

He wanted to get to the top and climbed on. The branches got smaller. Then his head bumped against something hidden in the big leaves.

Jay pushed them away and saw a board. He pushed the board, and it went up. When he took his hand away, it came down again.

"That's loose. I'd better be careful," he said. "But I'll have to get the board out of the way to climb any higher."

He pushed hard this time, and when the board went up, it did not come down. He could not see where it went, so he stuck his head up through the leaves. He saw a whole floor of boards. His head was in a hole in the floor.

Jay pulled himself through the hole and stood on the floor. All around he saw a low wall of boards and overhead a roof.

"A house—a tree house!" he said. "And that loose board is a trap door!"

There the board lay beside the hole. He saw an old box in the corner. There was nothing else in the tree house.

Jay walked around the wall trying to find a place where he could see through the leaves. At last he did and looked out over the low wall of the tree house. The cornfield was far below—to Jay it looked very, very far below.

"This is the highest tree house I've ever seen," he said.

Then he looked away to the end of the field at the barnyard. He saw his cousin Fred driving the tractor. It looked like a toy tractor. Fred was nearly a man, but he looked like a little boy way down there.

Everything looked small. The horses looked like ponies. The big goose flapping his wings looked like a little bird.

"What a lookout!" Jay said.

Then he heard his aunt Ellen call, "Ja-ay! Ja-ay! Where are you?"

"Here, Aunt Ellen! Here!" he called.

"Ja-ay! Ja-ay!" she called again.

Jay couldn't find a place where he could see the house.

He yelled as loud as he could, "Here-in-the-tree."

His aunt kept calling.

Jay laughed. "She can't hear me. Nobody can find me! This is a real hideout, all right."

But he thought he had better go.

He moved the trap door closer to the hole so he could reach up and shut it after he got through. There, behind the trap door, was a rope coiled up on the floor with big knots tied in it. Jay lifted the coil of rope, but it was very heavy and he dropped it.

One end fell through the hole of the trap door and slid down through the tree.

"Boy! What a long rope!" said Jay.

It stopped sliding, and he found out why it did. The end of the rope in the tree house was tied to a ring in the floor.

"I see—the fast way down! Watch out below!"

Down the rope went Jay, hand under hand,

with knees and feet holding to the knots. When he got to the end, he was still a little way from the ground, but not too far to drop.

Then he ran across the field to the house.

Aunt Ellen said, "Jay, I was calling you to dinner."

Just then Uncle Lester came in.

Jay told them about finding the tree house.

"Fred wanted you to find it by yourself," Aunt Ellen said, "for a surprise."

Uncle Lester said, "When he was about your age, I built that tree house for him."

"It's the highest one I ever saw!" Jay said.

"About twenty feet up," Uncle Lester said. "The tree is a horse chestnut—leaves about as big as they come."

Then Fred came in for dinner.

He said, "I saw you on the rope, Jay. I thought you could use one. It's new."

"Oh, I can, Fred. It's great!" said Jay.

"Fred still takes care of that tree house," Aunt Ellen said.

"I used to almost live in it," Fred said. "Now it's yours, Jay, while you're here."

"Boy! I'd like to live in it too. Could I eat there, Aunt Ellen?"

"Why—yes, Jay. Do you want to begin now—and take a lunch?" Aunt Ellen asked.

She did not wait for his answer, but made two sandwiches. Jay put them and an apple into his knapsack.

"An orange too?" he asked, taking one from a basket.

She nodded.

Jay hung the knapsack over his shoulder and ran back to the tree.

The Squirrel

This time he climbed the rope. It was harder to climb than the tree, but more fun. He could push one foot against the tree and swing. He could turn and twist. He could climb with his feet on the tree and his hands on the rope.

As Jay came up through the trap door, a swallow flew close to his head.

"Look out! Don't hit me!" he called. "What were you doing in here?"

The swallow flew over the low wall and away.

Jay saw that the floor was dirty with old leaves and nut shells and the box in the corner was full of leaves. He would have to bring up a broom and sweep.

He hung the knapsack on a nail on a post that held up the roof and took out a sandwich. He ate it *while* sitting on the wall.

Up here, on the wall, he could look out in more places. He saw Uncle Lester going into his tool shop. He saw the creek running beside the cornfield.

Then Jay walked along the top of the wall, holding on to the roof. Beyond the creek he saw a hill with woods.

"The higher I go, the more I can see," he said. "I'm going on the roof."

When he looked for a branch to climb up on, he saw a squirrel out in the tree. It was running from one branch to another. Sometimes it stopped and scolded, then it ran again, back and forth.

"Who are you scolding?" Jay called out. "I'm

your new neighbor."

He stepped out on the branch. As he did, a swallow flew by and almost hit him.

"I'm sure that's the same swallow," Jay said. "I

think it tried to hit me."

Close by he heard cheeping sounds. Up under the edge of the roof, he found a nest and saw little birds in it with their beaks wide open.

"Somebody is already living in this tree house," Jay said to himself.

"Was that swallow your mother?" he said to the little birds, and they cheeped louder.

He left the nest and climbed onto the roof. It was like a platform. From here he saw the house, the whole farm, the whole country.

Everywhere there was something to see. He could even see some of it sitting down. And when he lay on his back, he could see the whole sky.

For a long, long time he watched a cloud move and change its shape. He watched the sun going down, in and out among the clouds.

He lay still so long that the swallow flew past him into the tree house. Then another swallow did the same thing.

"Oh, there are two—the mother and the father. They have bugs in their bills. Now those babies will get something to eat," Jay said.

Then he remembered that all *he* had eaten was one sandwich. So he went down and ate the other one and took a bite of apple.

A sound came from across the floor. Over in

the corner on the old box, he saw the squirrel again. Now it had a baby squirrel in its mouth!

In one jump the mother was on the wall. In another jump she was in the tree. She ran behind a branch, and he couldn't see her again.

"More babies," Jay said, and laid the apple on the wall.

Then he looked into the box. The old leaves there were the outside of a nest. The inside was soft with grass and feathers. But it was empty.

"She's taking her baby away. I wish she had stayed," Jay said. "I am the one she was scolding. But we could all live here—the squirrels and the birds and I."

Jay didn't know if he could sleep in the tree house. He would ask Fred. Jay walked around the top of the wall looking for him and saw him in a hayfield driving the tractor.

Jay jumped to the floor and rushed down the rope. He was about to drop off the end when he saw an animal nearby in the cornfield. At first he thought it was a cat, but it took something off a corn plant with a hind foot.

Just as Jay dropped to the ground, he saw a rat tail on the animal. But when he looked again, the animal had gone.

Jay forgot about it by the time he got to Fred.

Fred said, "Why not sleep there? The two of us can get a sleeping bag up the tree—nothing to it."

The Swallows

After supper it was still light when Jay
and Fred went to the big tree. Jay carried
the sleeping bag and, in his pocket, some
dead beetles for the swallows. Fred carried a
flashlight and a coil of thin rope.

Fred climbed up and hung the rope over a
high branch above the tree house and let both
ends hang down to the ground. Jay tied one end
to the sleeping bag. Then he and Fred pulled on
the other end until the sleeping bag was all the
way up to the tree house.

Fred held the rope tight.

Jay climbed up into the tree house and pulled
his bed in, over the wall. Then he dropped the

end of the rope to Fred and called down, "The flashlight!"

Fred tied that to the rope, and Jay pulled it up to the tree house.

"Keep the rope; you may need it," Fred called up. "Goodnight!"

"Goodnight! Thanks!" Jay called down.

He made a coil of the thin rope and put it in a corner. He laid the trap door over the hole, against the big rope. He unrolled the sleeping bag. His pajamas were inside. So was a cowbell. Aunt Ellen had told him to ring it if he needed anything in the night.

Jay undressed and laid the flashlight and the bell where he could reach them in the dark.

It wasn't dark yet. He could see the white flowers of the tree. He saw the posts that held up the roof and the knapsack hanging on one of them. He could even see the apple he had laid on the wall. Then he remembered the orange he had not eaten.

He heard lots of noise from hundreds of frogs and a whip-poor-will. The swallows were quiet.

"I'll put out the beetles in the morning," Jay thought, as he fell asleep.

A loud noise woke him. He didn't know what it was nor where he was until he saw the bell lying on its side. Moonlight shone on the bell and on the white face of an animal.

It turned and walked away—slowly. Its legs were too short to walk fast. But it could surely climb! It climbed right up a post and over the wall. The last thing Jay saw was its rat-like tail.

"Why, that's the same animal that was in the cornfield," he said.

He got up and beamed his flashlight over the floor. In one place he saw an apple core. Near the bell he saw the knapsack and an orange that was partly eaten. Now he knew what had happened. The animal had been eating and had hit the bell.

Jay waited a long time, but the animal did not come back. From the nest a bird cheeped softly.

Jay went back to bed.

The next morning the baby swallows woke him. As he dressed, they cheeped loudly and stuck their heads out over the nest.

"Your parents must be hunting food," he said. "I'll put some on this branch for them."

He looked around for his shirt, to get the beetles out of the pocket, but it was not anywhere around—not on the floor, nor in his bed.

Maybe he had hung it over the wall and it had fallen into the tree. He couldn't see his shirt down below. Maybe it had fallen to the ground and he would find it there.

But he found it on the way down. The sleeves were hanging out of a hole in the dead branch.

Jay was on the rope and could not reach in that far. He pushed against the tree. The rope

swung out, then in toward the branch. He pulled the shirt. It was stuck in the hole.

Then it came loose. He heard hissing in the hole and tried to see in, but it was dark.

"Who are you in there—a snake?" he said.

Jay dropped his shirt to the ground, climbed into the tree, and let the rope go. Then he climbed back up and brought down his flashlight.

It shone on an animal with a long white face and a sharp pink nose. The animal yawned and yawned, showing very sharp teeth. Then it snorted and hissed at Jay.

He said, "You stole my shirt. You must be the fellow that ate my apple and my orange—and hit my bell. What animal are you?"

Later, at breakfast, Fred told Jay it was an opossum.

"What did it want with my shirt?" Jay asked.

"The beetles in it," Fred said. "Anyway, you can't feed swallows. They only eat the flying bugs they catch in the air."

"Could I tame the opossum?" Jay asked.

"Opossums don't tame very well," Fred said.

"Well, I could feed it anyway," said Jay.

"They feed at night," Fred said. "Come out about sundown."

"What do they eat besides apples and oranges?" Jay asked.

"Most anything—bugs, worms, frogs, birds—whatever they find," Fred said.

"Will it eat my swallows?" Jay asked.

"No danger of that. It can't climb upside down under the roof," said Fred.

The Opossums

Before sundown Jay was ready. On the dead branch outside the opossum's hole, he had laid an apple, a frog, some corn, strawberries, and bread. Then he sat above in the tree and watched.

The sun went down, and the light began to go out of the sky. The opossum did not come out, and Jay went home to supper.

When he came back, the moon was up and he could see that the food was gone.

For three afternoons Jay put out food. Each time he put it higher up in the tree so he could watch from the tree house. The food was always taken when he was away, and he never saw the opossum.

Many times during these three days, Jay used the thin rope.

He pulled up a broom. He pulled up a hammer and some boards. He wanted these to make steps on the tree where it was hard to climb.

He pulled up a basket. This he used for taking up small things—a can of nails, pieces of string, flashlight batteries, paper boxes to put things in.

Every night Jay slept in the tree house. He got tired of feeding an animal he never saw and stopped putting out food.

The swallows became used to him and fed their young when he was there.

One night as Jay came through the trap door, he beamed his flashlight around. There was the opossum! It was walking slowly across the floor.

Jay shut off the flashlight and stood still, against the wall. He did not know what the opossum would do.

The opossum went to the trap door and climbed out. It held on to the edge with its hind feet. They looked like hands to Jay because each one had a thumb, like his own. The opossum curled its tail around the rope and held on as it went through the hole.

"Come back tomorrow," Jay called down.

Thunder woke Jay during the night. There was lightning, and a big wind shook the tree. He felt the floor move. He heard the branches swish, then rain and hail on the roof.

He got out of bed to watch the storm. It was great. Again and again lightning cut the sky and thunder rolled and roared.

Then, from down below, he heard Fred yelling his name through the storm.

"Down the rope! Fast! Don't stop to dress!"

When Jay was down, Fred said, "Let's go!"

"But, Fred, I don't want a storm to run me out of the tree house. I want to stay."

"This tree might be hit by lightning," Fred said. "Quick—get away from it!"

He beamed a light ahead as they ran home.

The horse chestnut tree wasn't hit, but Jay found some branches on the ground the next morning. So many leaves had been blown off that he could see the tree house from below. It looked all right. Broken twigs and leaves were lying loose on the branches he had used for climbing. The big rope was twisted and tangled.

Jay cleaned out the tree and fixed the rope. When at last he got into the tree house, he first looked at the bird nest. The little swallows were there, calling for food as they did every day.

The floor of the house was wet and full of leaves and broken twigs. His sleeping bag was covered with them. It must be wet, too. He began to clean off the bag.

As he took up the leaves, he felt something move in his hands. Inside them was what looked like a tiny baby mouse. Strangely, it did not run but only looked at him with large black eyes.

He heard grunting from his bed. The opossum! It was lying among the leaves there.

On top of its head sat another baby mouse like
the one in Jay's hands. Then he saw more of
them.

"Opossum babies!" he said.

He put the one he held back on the bed. The
mother opened her mouth and snapped at him.
He sat on the wall to watch. She licked and

washed her babies. Then she slept. So did the babies, close beside her. Jay counted them—five.

He cleaned up his floor. Whenever he looked at the opossum, she was still sleeping.

"I did invite you, Mrs. Opossum, but only for a visit," he said. "Why don't you sleep in your own house? I've got to dry out my bed."

He got a stick and poked at her to wake her up. Again she snapped at him. The babies began to crawl. Jay backed away. One crawled toward him. He picked it up and two of the others.

"I'll take you to your house, and maybe your mother will go home."

He put the little opossums in his pockets and climbed down to the dead branch.

It was not there! The wind had broken it off. So Jay went back up and put the babies on his bed.

"I guess we have to live in the same house, Mrs. Opossum," he said.

About dark Jay watched the opossum leave the tree house by herself. But he could not find the babies. He looked in his bed and in the old box. They were not in the tree house.

His sleeping bag was too wet and dirty to sleep in. It would have to be washed. So he took it home and slept there in a bed.

The next morning he found the opossum sleeping in the squirrel nest in the box—and two babies were with her.

The mother was on her side with the two babies lying on her stomach. Then Jay saw a strange thing happen. Another baby crawled out of a hole in the mother's stomach—then another and another, and more kept coming! Jay counted seven.

"So that's where she hides you!" Jay said. "Just like a kangaroo!"

Nine babies in all. For a little while, they climbed around—on their mother and all over the box. Then they went close to her and slept. Some went back into her pocket.

"If we're going to live in the same house, Mrs. Opossum, I may as well feed you here," Jay said. "Anyway, you've found a bed, and now I can bring mine back."

But when Jay did, the opossum slept on it.
Now that she didn't have to hunt all her food,
she stayed home until late at night.

Jay had to give up sleeping in the tree house.

The Roof

The little opossums grew too big to fit in their mother's pocket. So they rode on her when she went hunting. Each one hung on to her fur wherever it could—on her back, her sides, her head.

The mother never became tame, but she let Jay pet the little ones. They were not afraid of him. Sometimes he would find one asleep in his pocket. They were fun to watch. After they ate, they washed their toes and whiskers.

In the tree house, they climbed everywhere and used their tails to hold on. The only place they couldn't climb was up under the roof. Fred was right. The swallows were safe.

They found Jay's lunch even when he hung it high up on a post. So Jay ate at home.

Their sharp little teeth chewed at everything—his string, his paper boxes, even his basket. So Jay took these things home.

Their hand-like feet picked up his small

things and often dropped them over the wall.
So Jay took these things home, too.

At last he stopped bringing food for the
opossums. He wanted the mother to find a
home of her own. But she stayed on.

"Whose tree house is it?" Fred asked one day.

"Right now it's the opossums," Jay said. "It
seems as if I'll never get to live in it."

One hot morning when Jay came to the tree
house, the little swallows had left the nest.

"I wish I had seen them fly out," he said.

The opossums were asleep in the old box.

Jay climbed up on the roof. At least that part
of the tree house was his. The opossums would
not come there in the sun.

A small wind cooled Jay's hot face. He saw
that there was no wind down in the cornfield.
The leaves hung still.

If he had a windmill up here, he could look at it from the ground and see when the wind blew. Maybe Uncle Lester would let him make one in the shop.

One of the parent swallows was calling and

flying back and forth. A little one was sitting on a branch below the roof. The parent chirped and called. The little one teetered back and forth. The other parent flew past it with a bug, trying to coax the baby to fly.

Jay called, "Don't be afraid, little fellow."

At last it flew. He couldn't see where it went, but the parents flew under the roof. They chirped very fast and louder than ever.

Jay rushed down. When he got on the wall of the tree house, he saw the old opossum climb out of the box. There on the floor was the baby swallow lying on its back. It had fallen.

The opossum ran toward the little bird.

Jay jumped off the wall and ran to the opossum. He grabbed her tail and pulled. She fell and lay still. Her eyes closed and her mouth opened and her tongue hung out.

Jay pulled a little on her tail. She did not seem to feel it. He lifted her a little by the tail, but she hung down very still. He let go. There she lay with her tongue out and her eyes closed. He pushed her with his foot. She felt like a rag.

"Why, she is dead," Jay said. "Poor thing."

Then he picked up the swallow.

It was alive; its heart beat against his fingers. So he held it awhile and then carried it to the roof. Up there it tried to get out of his hand. He set it down, and it hopped on a twig.

Jay waited awhile, watching, until the parents came with food.

"You're all right now. But the little opossums have no mother. I'll have to dig a grave for her, then take care of them," Jay said.

When he got back in the tree house, the opossum was not there! Who could have taken her away? He looked in the box. The little ones were gone, too. But she was dead—surely she *was* dead.

"She was playing opossum!" Uncle Lester said when Jay told him about it later, down at the shop. "You scared her, and she's gone for good."

"Now it's my tree house!" Jay said, and then asked if he could make the windmill.

"Well, well. I guess there's no end to what you can do with a tree house," Uncle Lester said. "Sure you can. I'll have my job off the workbench this morning, and you can begin yours this afternoon—if it's not too hot to work."

Jay looked at the thermometer on the door. "Ninety now," he said. "It's not too hot for me."

"Would that thermometer be any use to you, Jay?"

"Oh, yes, Uncle Lester! I could tell how hot it is in the tree house. And if I put a can on the roof to catch rain, I could measure the rain."

Uncle Lester said, "That's right—you could."

Jay went on, "And with the windmill, first thing you know, I'll have a weather station at the tree house! Boy! I'm going to get the basket and put my things in it and move back right now!"

*Rags—An Orphan of the Storm
and Other Animal Stories*
by Various Authors

David and the Seagulls
by Marion Downer

Mr. Apple's Family
by Jean McDevitt

Brian's Victory
by Ethel Calvert Phillips